YOU'VE GOT
A FRIEND,
CHARLIE BROWN

by Charles M. Schulz

Selected Cartoons from
You'll Flip, Charlie Brown, Vol. 1

A FAWCETT CREST BOOK
Fawcett Publications, Inc., Greenwich, Conn.

YOU'VE GOT A FRIEND, CHARLIE BROWN

This book, prepared especially for Fawcett Publications, Inc.,
comprises the first half of YOU'LL FLIP, CHARLIE BROWN, and
is reprinted by arrangement with Holt, Rinehart & Winston, Inc.

WELL, I'LL PROBABLY NEED A HALF DOZEN FUR COATS, AT LEAST THIRTY SKI OUTFITS AND ABOUT FIFTY FORMALS... I'LL NEEDS LOTS OF JEWELRY AND EXOTIC PERFUMES AND I'LL NEED ABOUT A HUNDRED PAIRS OF SHOES...

WE'LL HAVE TO HAVE A SWIMMING POOL, OLYMPIC SIZE, HEATED, AND RIDING HORSES, A TENNIS COURT AND A HUGE FORMAL GARDEN... WE WILL TRAVEL EXTENSIVELY, OF COURSE; ROUND-THE-WORLD CRUISES... THAT SORT OF THING... AND...

KEEP PRACTICING, KID!

I CAN'T SLEEP!

MAYBE IF I MOVE AROUND AND TRY DIFFERENT POSITIONS...

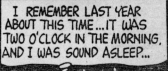

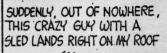

ARE YOU GOING TO BE A NEWSPAPER BOY WHEN YOU GET OLDER, CHARLIE BROWN?

WELL, I'D LIKE TO BE... YES, I THINK I'D LIKE TO HAVE MY OWN ROUTE..

THEN YOU SHOULD LEARN HOW TO ROLL AND FOLD A PAPER SO YOU CAN TOSS IT ONTO A DOOR STEP...HERE, LET ME SHOW YOU...

IT'S FAIR WEATHER TODAY, CHARLIE BROWN..

SO WHERE ARE ALL MY FRIENDS?

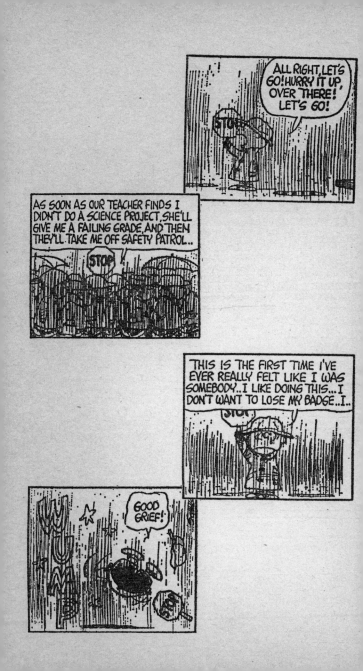

NOW Peanuts Jewelry

Each item is 14 Kt. gold finish, hand-crafted cloisonné in brilliant colors, exquisitely designed by Aviva. Items shown in actual size. Complete satisfaction guaranteed or money refunded.

No. 10 pin $3

No. 11 pin $3

No. 12 pin $3

No. 13A pierced $3
No. 13B non-pierced $3

No. 14 pin $3

No. 15 pin $3

No. 16 pin $3

No. 17A pierced $3
No. 17B non-pierced $3

No. 18 pin $3

No. 19 pin $3

© United Feature Syndicate, Inc. 1971

No. 20 pin $3

No. 21 pin $3

More Peanuts Jewelry
See Previous Page

No. 22 tie tack $3

No. 23 tie tack $3

No. 24 key chain $3

No. 25 money clip $4

No. 26 tie tack $3

No. 27 tie bar $3

No. 28 cufflinks $4

No. 29 pin $3

Please specify identity number of each item ordered and add 25¢ for each item to cover postage and handling. Personal check or money order. No cash. Send orders to HAMILTON HOUSE, Cos Cob, Conn. 06807.